Oscar S. (Oscar Solomon) Straus

Religious Liberty in the United States

Oscar S. (Oscar Solomon) Straus

Religious Liberty in the United States

ISBN/EAN: 9783337129187

Printed in Europe, USA, Canada, Australia, Japan

Cover: Foto ©ninafisch / pixelio.de

More available books at **www.hansebooks.com**

Religious Liberty
In the United States

By

OSCAR S. STRAUS

FORMER UNITED STATES MINISTER TO TURKEY
AUTHOR OF " ROGER WILLIAMS THE PIONEER
OF RELIGIOUS LIBERTY"
"THE ORIGIN OF REPUBLICAN FORM OF GOVERNMENT
IN THE UNITED STATES "

و%

An address delivered before the
Yale College Kent Club, New Haven
Contemporary Club, Philadelphia
Y. M. H. A., New York

NEW YORK: 1896
PHILIP COWEN, PUBLISHER
213-215 E. 44TH STREET

Religious Liberty in the United States

*** ***

THE spirit of patriotism is kindled on the altars of our national history. " Few greater calamities," says Lecky, " can befall a nation than to cut herself off, as France did in her great Revolution, from all vital connection with her own past." History is to a nation what experience is to an individual, and just as a wise man will guide himself by "the lamp of experience," so will a patriotic people run not after strange gods, but will direct their course under the guidance of the philosophy of their own past. Fortunately, our national history is a legible book which the dust of ages has not obliterated, so that it cannot be said of our past, as Gibbon said in speaking of the first thousand years of the British Empire, that it was "familiar to the most ignorant and obscure to the most learned."

In the heat of party and sectional controversies of the day, we are too apt to forget that the liberties we enjoy did not spring into existence spontaneously and full-grown, but were the fruit of a gradual and logical development, whose roots run far into the past experience of the nations of the old world from whom came the early settlers who composed the thirteen original colonies. These colonists brought with them their national traits, which is but another name for the reflex of national experience upon personal character. They brought with them their religious beliefs and aspirations, which were intensified by a sense of martyrdom because of persecutions they had suffered in their native lands. In the days of Brewster, of Winthrop, of Calvert and of Penn, America was not an inviting country either for permanent abode or as a place of recreation; nor did it offer attractions to pleasure-seekers. It required some strong inducements for men with their wives and children to brave the dangers of the sea and the still greater dangers and hardships that awaited them on land. But for those inducements the development of our continent would have been delayed and it would have continued for many years to serve as trading posts for English and Dutch merchants, and as Europe's Siberia.

Colonization in all ages was due either to conquest, to commerce or to causes of conscience. The great extension of the Greek and Roman empires under Alexander and Cæsar arose out of the first of these causes. The great power of the Venetian republic in the thirteenth century was owing to its commercial spirit. The early colonization of North America is chiefly to be attributed to causes of conscience. Persecution has ever been an active colonizer, and has usually supplied an element well adapted for the purpose of building up a cultured and enlightened community. In every age it was not the worst, but, according to the real measure of worth, rather the best among a people who,

true to their consciences, sacrificed their tempo-
ral advantages upon the altar of their faith.

The cradle of religious liberty has been
rocked by the worst passions of mankind. Until
comparatively recent times, every sect was intolerant from conviction, and held it as a sacred
duty to banish or burn the unrepentant heretics.
Even heretics, when they became dominant, were
not less intolerant toward their former orthodox
persecutors. Do unto others as others have done
unto you was the rule of persecutors. Heresy,
whatever it may signify ecclesiastically, was his-
torically the penalty for dissent exacted by the
State religion from conscientious sectaries. " I
never knew the time in England," said Milton,
" when men of truest religion were not counted
sectaries."

In the United States liberty of worship and
of belief in matters of religion is not a concession
or a privilege ; it is a fundamental right recognized as being inherent in every individual, and
the federal government is pledged not to abridge
it or in any wise interfere therewith. This is the

signification of our national constitution. Had the Constitution remained silent upon the sub-ject, religious liberty would still have existed under and by reason of it; yet, in that event, what would have been the subject of construction has been placed beyond cavil or dispute, so that even if a less liberal spirit should prevail, Con-gress could not assume the right to legislate sec-tarianism, Protestantism, Romanism, or any form of religion into civil life. The statesmen who framed our Constitution were too well read in the history of other governments, and had before them too clearly the sufferings of the people in their colonial state, not to dread and anticipate the abuse of authority resulting from the greed of power and the selfishness of sects, so they wisely guarded against this contingency by express enactment, whereby it is provided that " No reli-gious test shall ever be required as a qualification to any office or public trust under the United States."

When the Constitution was submitted for ratification to the several states, considerable uneasiness was manifested at the failure of Mr. Pinckney's resolution in the Federal Convention, that " The Legislature of the United States shall pass no law on the subject of religion ; " and upon ratifying the instrument, the New Hampshire, New York and Virginia conventions urged the adoption of an amendment to that effect.

The conventions of the several states which were held in 1777 and 1778 reflected the conflicting sentiments then entertained on the question of religious tests.   The exclusion of such tests as a qualification for public office was opposed in those states which required such tests, under the fear that, without them, the Federal Government might pass into the hands of Roman Catholics, Jews or infidels.   It was alleged that, as the Constitution stood, the Pope of Rome might become President of the United States, and there was even a pamphlet printed stating that objection. In the North Carolina Convention, a spirited debate occurred, and Mr. James Iredell, the leader of the Federalists, and afterwards by Washington appointed on the Supreme Court Bench, referring to the subject, said : " I met by accident with a pamphlet this morning in which the author states there is a very serious danger that the Pope might be elected President. I confess this never struck me before, and if the author had read all the qualifications of a President, perhaps his fear might have been quieted. No man but a native, or who has resided fourteen years in America, can be chosen President. I know not all the qualifications for Pope, but I believe he must be taken from the College of Cardinals, and probably there are many previous steps necessary before he arrives at this dignity. A native American must have very singular good fortune who, after residing fourteen years in his own country, should come to Europe, enter Romish orders, obtain the promotion of cardinal, afterward that of Pope, and at length be so much in the confidence of his country as to be elected President. It would be still more extraordinary," continues Mr. Iredell, " if he should give up his popedom for our presidency."

On the other hand, while several states adopted the constitution, the majority in their respective conventions had the apprehension that the clause of the constitution, above quoted, did not go far enough, and therefore they proposed amendments guaranteeing religious freedom and other fundamental rights. The strongest opposition to the abolition of religious tests was in Massachusetts, where Congregationalism was the established church ; and the greatest apprehension that the exclusion of religious tests, as contained in the constitution, was insufficient and that a more explicit guarantee against the establishment of religion was demanded, was in Virginia and Rhode Island. The first Congress of the United States met in the city of New York under the constitution on March 4th, 1789. In the session of June 8th, the House of Representatives, on motion of James Madison of Virginia, took into consideration the amendments to the constitution desired by the several states.   Mr. Madison moved the appointment of a select committee to report preliminary amendments, and supported the motion by a forcible speech, urging as a reason chiefly the duty of Congress to remove all apprehensions of an intention to deprive the people "of the liberty for which they valiautly fought and honorably bled." Congress accordingly sent twelve amendments to the Legislatures of the several states for ratification. Of these, ten were duly ratified. The first of these is the clause, "Congress shall make no law respecting an establishment of religion or prohibiting the free exercise thereof."*

---

* JEFFERSON TO DOCTOR PRIESTLY.

WASHINGTON, June 19, 1802.

I was in Europe when the Constitution was planned, and never saw it till after it was established. On receiving it, I wrote strongly to Mr. Madison, urging the want of provision for the freedom of religion, freedom of the press, trial by jury, habeas corpus, the substitution of militia for a standing army, and an express reservation to the States of all rights not specifically granted to the Union. He accordingly moved in the first session of Congress for these amendments, which were agreed to and ratified by the States as they now stand.

Jefferson's Works, Vol. 4, p. 441. Washington, 1854.

Brief as these two provisions of our Constitution are, they proclaim religious liberty in its
broadest acceptation as the fundamental right of
every American, be he citizen or alien. By
incorporating these provisions in their constitution; the American people were the first to set
the world the example of entirely separating the
institution which has for its object the support
of religion from its political government.

Before the Revolution the dominant sects in
the various colonies were distributed as follows :
The Puritans in Massachusetts, the Baptists in
Rhode Island, the Congregationalists in Connecticut ; the Dutch and Swedish Protestants in
New Jersey ; the Anglicans in New York ; the
Quakers in Pennsylvania ; the Catholics in Baltimore ; the Cavaliers in Virginia ; the Baptists,
Methodists, Quakers and Presbyterians, in North
Carolina ; the Huguenots and Episcopalians in
South Carolina, and the Methodists in Georgia.
With the exception of Pennsylvania, Maryland,
and Rhode Island, some form of religious establishment had existed in all other colonies.

Let us tarry a moment in Rhode Island, the land where the banner of religious liberty was first unfurled. In the middle of winter, 1636, a solitary pilgrim might have been seen wandering through the primeval forests of New England, an exile from the territory of the Massachusetts Puritans, seeking a place of refuge from ecclesiastical tyranny, where he and all men might worship God according to the dictates of their consciences. At that time throughout the whole civilized world there was no such land. The colonists of Virginia were strict conformists to the rites of the Church of England. There was less freedom there than in England. The settled portions of New England were domineered over by the Puritans and Pilgrim Fathers, who had left their English homes to escape ecclesiastical tyranny only to set up a greater tyranny of their own. This pilgrim, the first true type of an American freeman, the trusted and trustworthy friend of the savage Indian, the benefactor of all mankind, was Roger Williams, who accomplished what no one before this ever had the courage and wisdom, combined with the conviction of the broadest liberty, even to attempt : to found a purely secular state "as a shelter for the poor and the persecuted according to their several persuasions."

The time, let us hope, is not far off, when the civilized people, in the remotest corners of the world, will recognize the truth and power of the principles which throw around the name of Roger Williams a halo of imperishable glory and fame. So great was the hatred felt towards this " heretic colony" that Massachusetts passed a law prohibiting the inhabitants of Providence from coming' within her bounds.

It is not surprising that the Roman Catholics, who in Protestant England were proscribed as a class, should eagerly direct their eyes to the new world for a place of refuge. Lord Baltimore had become a devout convert to Romanism. By reason of his high official position and his being in the good graces of James I., he succeeded in obtaining a charter for Maryland which embodied a very broad conception of toleration. There

was no limitation on the freedom of conscience
save only that Christianity was made the law of
the land. This was a great step in the direction
of full liberty in matters of religion, and a century
in advance of his time, or of the New England
colonies and Virginia. The same reasons which
impelled the Pilgrims, the Puritans, and the
Catholics to look to the western continent as a
harbor of refuge from ecclesiastical tyranny,
operated with increased force upon the Quakers,
who were exposed to almost universal persecution, hatred and contempt not only by the
prelatical party, but also by the dissenters. The
laws agreed upon in England for their government in Pennsylvania provided for equal toler-
ance of all sects and creeds that recognized a
deity, whereby both Jew and Gentile were to be
protected in belief and in form of worship. These
laws went a step farther than those of Maryland
in their approach to religious liberty, yet not so
far as those of Rhode Island, as rationalists and
atheists were discriminated against. The colonists, however, shortly after the arrival of Wil-

liam Penn, took a backward step, showing that
Penn's followers were not as liberal as he, for by
the enactments known as the "Great Law of
Chester," agreed upon in 1682, religious toleration was curtailed, by providing that all the
officers of the colony should be only such as
professed belief in the Christian religion.

The perpetual strife which had existed in
England between the prelatical party and the
Puritans was not of such a nature as to engender
toleration. The entire contention was about
ceremonies and, great as the sufferings of the
Puritans had been, when they succeeded to power,
they did not rise to the height of a principle,
but were content to rest on the plane of their
persecutors. The Puritans who sought New
England were not actuated altogether by humane
or liberal motive. They sought liberty of worship for themselves and for themselves only, they
appropriated the land of the Indians, and then
slaughtered them when driven to rebellion, all
dissenting Christians whom they could not con-
vince they exiled and some even they executed

in cold blood ; in their eyes toleration was a heresy and liberty was a crime.

The Virginia colonists, on the other hand, were neither exiles nor refugees. They did not come to the shores of Virginia to organize liberty or to Christianize the heathens, but to dig gold and cultivate tobacco. A story is told of an official, to whom a Virginia delegation had commended a measure for the good of the souls, replying, " damn your souls, grow tobacco."

Their first charter is evidence that they were nothing more nor less than a mercantile corporation of the South Sea bubble phase, of which the King was the head, and whereover he reserved absolute legislative authority with the hope of an ultimate revenue. " Religion was established according to the doctrine and the rites of the Church of England within the realm, and no emigrant might avow dissent or affect the superstitions of the Church of Rome or withdraw his allegiance from King James."

It is plainly evident that neither the Anglicans of Virginia nor the Puritans of New England, both of whom had modeled their civil polity to conserve state-churchism, were likely to advance the cause of religious liberty, if left to themselves, as they hoped to be ; on the contrary, their aims and efforts, as evinced by their laws and regulations, were directed to achieve the opposite result. The rise of that liberty, which was destined to illume the Western world, must be searched for elsewhere, and whatever credit rightly belongs to these two sects arises from their violent efforts to repress, not to establish liberty in matters of conscience. Here, as in all communities, liberty came creeping in with the dissenting minorities.

Passing over the intermediate evidences of intolerance embodied in the early laws and regulations of the various colonies, let us examine, for a moment, the constitutions of several of the colonies in respect to religion just prior to the framing of our national constitution, which afford a striking illustration of the intolerance of the various sects then dominant. Congregationalism still continued to be the established religion in

Massachusetts, New Hampshire and Connecticut. The Church of England had the civil support in all the southern colonies, and partially in New York and New Jersey. In Massachusetts the Legislature expressly authorized and impliedly required compulsory attendance at church and the civil support of the ministers. Heavy penalties were prescribed against all who might question the divine inspiration of any book of the New or Old Testament, and the old laws against blasphemy were revived. Similar laws remained in force in Connecticut, and were re-enacted in New Hampshire. By the second constitution of South Carolina, Protestantism was declared to be the established religion of the state. The constitution of Maryland contained authority to levy a general and equal tax for the support of the Christian religion. In several of the states religious tests for public office were still retained. In New Hampshire, New Jersey, North Carolina, South Carolina and Georgia, the chief officers of the state were required to be Protestants. In Massachusetts and in Maryland all office-holders were required to declare their belief in the Christian religion. In South Carolina they must believe in a future state of rewards and punishment. In North Carolina and Pennsylvania they were required to acknowledge the inspiration of the New and the Old Testament, and in Delaware to believe in the Trinity.

The agitation for the overthrow of the established church and for complete separation of Church and State was first begun and successfully effected in Virginia, a state where we would least have expected it, where the church was most closely allied with the civil powers, where it was most firmly seated and had more privileges than elsewhere, and where its restrictions upon dissenters were most exacting. By the several acts of the Virginia Assembly, it was made penal in parents to refuse to have their children baptized. They had prohibited as unlawful the assembling of Quakers, and such as were within the colony were subject to imprisonment until they should abjure the country, and on their third return they were liable to the penalty of death.

Under the guiding spirit of Thomas Jefferson, the first Assembly of Virginia repealed all such obnoxious laws as were still on the statute books. He continued his onslaught upon the established church for more than nine years, assisted by Patrick Henry and James Madison and the leaders of the more liberal sects, until the problem of religious liberty was solved in all its completeness. "These nine years of Virginia's debates," says the biographer of Jefferson, "have perished, but something of their heat and strenuous vigor survives in his 'Notes on Virginia,' written towards the end of the Revolutionary War, and circulated a year before the final triumph of religious freedom." These vigorous utterances were the arsenal from which the advocates of religious liberty drew their weapons for the space of fifty years until the last remaining union between Church and State was severed. "Opinion," said Mr. Jefferson, "is something with which the government has nothing to do. It does me no injury for my neighbor to say there are twenty gods or no god. It is error alone which needs the support of government; truth can stand by itself. Millions of innocent men, women and children since the introduction of Christianity have been burnt, tortured, fined and imprisoned, yet we have not advanced an inch toward uniformity. What has been the effect? To make one-half the world fools and the other half hypocrites."

That the passage of the act for the establishment of religious liberty, together with the arguments contained in the "Notes on Virginia," had a far-reaching effect and great weight in the Federal Convention which assembled in May, 1787, at the city of Philadelphia for the purpose of framing a constitution, can scarcely be doubted, especially when we take into consideration that Virginia was the banner state, represented in the convention by Madison and Mason, both of whom had been collaborators with Jefferson.

The separation of Church and State, impelled by the example of Virginia and by the national constitution, gradually spread from state to state until the last link was severed and the union was forever broken. Many, who have not taken the trouble to examine this subject, are under the impiession that by the adoption of the constitution the union between Church and State was severed throughout the United States. So far as the national government is concerned, that is true in the sense that they never were united; but as regards the state governments, each was left free to legislate upon the subject of religion as it might determine, and the result was, as we have seen, that in several of the New England states the Church continued to be united with the State for many years, and to be supported by it. The last state which required a religious test for office was that of New Hampshire, whose constitution, adopted in 1792, provided that no one, unless he is of the Protestant religion, shall be eligible to the office of Governor, or to either house of the Legislature. The reason that this old provision remained until 1877 in the constitution was due doubtless to the fact that the exclusion was a dead letter and was not of practical consequence.

It is a cause of congratulation that America has given the world at large and the governments of Europe proof of the fact, by actual trial, that neither Church nor State is benefited by being united ; on the contrary, they both flourish best in the atmosphere of freedom.*

If we were to single out the men who from the beginning of our colonial state until the present time have most eminently contributed to

---

*JEFFERSON TO JAMES MADISON.
PARIS, December 16, 1786.

" The Virginia act for religious freedom has been received with infinite approbation in Europe, and propagated with enthusiasm, I do not mean by the governments, but by the individuals who compose them. It has been translated into French and Italian, has been sent to most of the courts of Europe, and has been the best evidence of the falsehood of those reports which stated us to be in anarchy. It is inserted in the new Encyclopedie, and is appearing in most of the publications respecting America. In fact, it is comfortable to see the standard of reason at length erected, after so many ages, during which the human mind has been held in vassalage by kings, priests and nobles, and it is honorable for us to have produced the first legislature who had the courage to declare that the reason of man may be trusted with the formation of his own opinions."

Jefferson's Works, Vol. 2, p. 67. 1853, Washington, D. C.

fostering and securing religious freedom, who have made this country of ours the haven of refuge from ecclesiastical tyranny and persecution, who have set an example more puissant than army or navy for freeing the conscience of men from civil interference, and have leavened the mass of intolerance wherever the name of America is known, I would mention first the Baptist, Roger Williams, who maintained the principle that the civil powers have no right to meddle in matters of conscience, and who founded a state with that principle as its keystone.   I would mention second the Catholic, Lord Baltimore, the proprietor of Maryland, to whom belongs the credit of having established liberty in matters of worship which was second only to Rhode Island. I would name third the Quaker, Penn, whose golden motto was "We must yield the liberties we demand." Fourth on the list is Thomas Jefferson, that "arch infidel," as he has been termed by some religious writers, who overthrew the established church in his own state, and then, with prophetic statesmanship, made it imposssible for any church to establish itself under our national constitution or in any way to abridge the rights of conscience.

There are many other bright names in our history, such as Henry, Mason, Madison and Franklin, who contributed to the same good end, besides the champions who led the victory in the various states, among whom were many devout and learned ministers of the several denominatious.

" Religious liberty," in the language of Mr. Thomas F. Bayard, when Secretary of State, " is the chief corner stone of the American system of government, and provisions for its security are imbedded in the written charter and interwoven in the moral fabric of our laws. Anything that tends to invade a right so essential and sacred must be carefully guarded against, and I am satisfied that my countrymen, ever mindful of the sufferings and sacrifices necessary to obtain it, will never consent to its impairment for any reason or under any pretext whatever."

The claim has at times been made by bigoted fanatics who would subvert the grand charter of our liberties to serve their selfish purposes, that this is a Christian country in the sense that Protestant Christianity is the basis of our system of government, and that the rights of Catholics, Jews and Free-thinkers need not be considered. This claim is usually made for the purpose of so amending our Constitution as to establish what they believe to be a Christian government.

For awhile, in support of this, the claim was made that such was the intent of the framers of the Constitution. In proof they cited the fact that, during the sitting of the Federal Convention, at a time when it was feared that its labors could not be brought to a successful close, even Franklin proposed to call in the clergymen of Philadelphia, to request them to preface the sessions with prayers. Some writers have questioned Franklin's sincerity in making this motion. Apart from doubt as to the purpose of Mr. Franklin in making this motion, it was not put to a vote, and no prayers were said either before, during or after the sitting of this convention. Franklin states "the convention, except three or four persons, thought prayers unnecessary."

After the adoption of the Constitution on the 4th of November, 1796, during the Presidency of Washington, a treaty was concluded with Tripoli, which was ratified by the Senate, under the presidency of John Adams, on June 7th, 1797, wherein it is provided : "As the government of the United States is not in any sense founded on the Christian religion ; as it has itself no character of enmity against the laws, religion or tranquility of Mussulmen. . . it is declared by the parties that no pretext arising from religious opinions shall ever produce an interruption of harmony existing between the two countries." " This declaimer by Washington," says Rev. Dr. Samuel T. Spear, one of our ablest writers on constitutional law, "in negotiating and by the Senate in confirming the treaty with Tripoli, was not designed to disparage the Christian religion, or indicate any hostility thereto, but to set forth the fact, so apparent in the Constitution itself, that the government of the United States was not founded upon that religion, and hence did not embody or assert any of its doctrines. The language of this article in the treaty was used for a purpose, and that purpose was in exact correspondence with the fact as contained in the Constitution itself. Christianity, though the prevalent religion of the people when the Constitution was adopted, is unknown to it."

This subject has been in some form or other before the courts in several states, and nowhere more directly at issue and more learnedly considered than in the case of Minor against the Board of Education of the City of Cincinnati. The School Board was represented by George Hoadley, late Governor of Ohio; Stanley Matthews, afterwards Associate Justice of the United States Supreme Court, and by Judge Stallo, later Minister to Italy. Judge Stallo, in a most scholarly presentation of the entire question, addressing himself to the claim made by the plaintiffs that Christianity was a part of the law of the State, concluded in these words : " Christianity was part of the law of Massachusetts two hundred and thirty years ago when Roger Williams was cited before the General Court for preaching the doctrine of liberty of conscience, and was sent into the wilderness in midwinter for that offence, when Quakers were banished and Quakeresses hanged; it was part of the law of the State of New York, where the penalty of death was threatened to be inflicted on Catholic priests for bringing the sacrament to the dying faithful; it was part of the common law of Virginia, where dissenters were required to build the churches of the Anglicans ; but it is not to-day part of the common law of Ohio, or, indeed, of any state in the Union I know of."*

Mr. Lecky, in his "Rationalism in Europe," says : "In one age the persecutor burnt the heretic : in another he crushed him with penal laws; in a third he withheld from him places of emolument; in a fourth he subjected him to the excommunication of society. Each stage of advancing toleration marks a stage of the decline of the spirit of dogmatism and of the increase of the spirit of truth."

* See article by Louis Marshall, " Is Ours a Christian Country ?" *The Menorah*, January, 1896.

That there are vestiges and distinct traces of this infection even at this day in our own country, I need scarcely point out. The people in this country through severe trials and conflicts have successfully expelled from their civil polity all distinctions of creed and caste, in consonance with the great declaration of the men of '76, that all men are created equal. And they did this in the face of the governments and the customs of the civilized world, at a time when under all forms of polity the relations which men bore to one another rested upon distinctions of birth and privileges established by law, at a time when democracy, such as they organized, based upon manhood suffrage was looked upon as the dream of the theorist, suitable only to the wild Indian dwelling in pristine barbarism. On these broad and humane principles and by reason thereof the American people have built up a nation and achieved a prosperity which outstrips the pro-phecies of her most enthusiastic admirers. They have done this in the face of ancient and hered-itary prejudices that were as old and as firmly set

as the pyramids. It is especially fitting, aye, more
than that, it is the duty of every American man
and woman to free their own minds from ancient
hatred and hereditary prejudices, and to instil in
the minds of their children the humane principles that underlie our civil State. Let them bear
in mind that just so sacred as religion is, so is
every one's right to choose the one by which his
hopes and his aspirations shall be guided, and
that every distinction and proscription based upon the denial of this sacred right is as much in
conflict with true religion as with true democracy.

Hon. J. L. M. Curry, in his valuable essay,
" Establishment and Disestablishment," very cor-
rectly says: " In the United States, it cannot be too
frequently or strongly reaffirmed, churches or
denominations or sects are on a plane of undistin-
guishable equality before law. The government
cannot interfere with their doctrines, discipline,
worship, or the appointment or support of the
clergy. It is sheer impertinence, insolent assump-
tion, to talk of any American citizens as Dissenters

or Non-conformists, or for any denomination to arrogate to itself the name of ' The Church of the United States,' or for any ecclesiastical functionary to sign himself ' the Bishop of Pennsylvania,' or of any other state. The Constitution, the political idea, the civil policy, of the United States, know no church or denomination; and, for convenience sake or from wrong use of words, we have adopted such phraseology as ' Divorce of Church and State, Alliance of Church and State. ' "

The spirit that guided the work of the founders of our government was not one that was crushed and screwed into sectarian molds by the decrees of intolerant councils and by the subtleties of ingenious priests—it recognizes the value of every creed, but rises above them all. The grand and noble purpose was 'to establish justice, promote the general welfare, and secure the blessings of liberty to ourselves and our posterity.'

This is the lesson of the development of civil as well as religious liberty in the United States.

Read it and indeed enjoyed S. W. Nichis

www.ingramcontent.com/pod-product-compliance
Lightning Source LLC
Chambersburg PA
CBHW061239260626
47172CB00003B/931